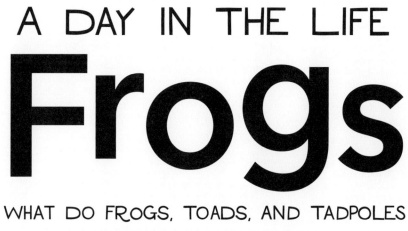

A DAY IN THE LIFE
Frogs

WHAT DO FROGS, TOADS, AND TADPOLES
GET UP TO ALL DAY?

NEON SQUID

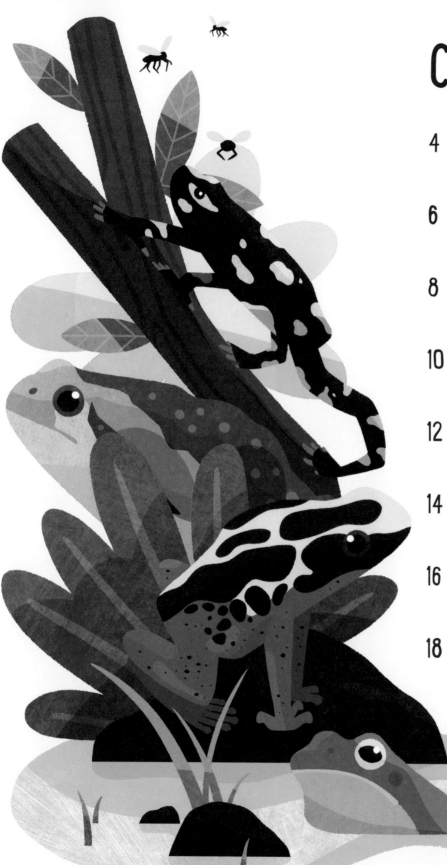

Contents

Welcome to the world of frogs!

Imagine you are standing in the middle of the forest at night, looking at the moon. The shadows of the trees are moving and the frogs are calling for one another ("croak, croak, croak"). That is my **happy place**.

When I was growing up, I did not know much about frogs at all. But then one day at college I was doing fieldwork at night when I met a tree frog. To me, holding this frog felt like holding **my best friend's hand**—I had an overwhelming feeling of love, and I wanted to learn everything I could about frogs!

When frogs look at me with their big bright eyes, I feel like they have secrets to tell me. As a **herpetologist** (frog scientist) it is my job to discover these secrets. But I could not do it all by myself—science is a team effort! The stories in this book were inspired by the work of biologists all over the world.

While we sleep, frogs are out and about doing **amazing things**—so much of this book takes place at night. We will see frogs making their own medicine, eating snakes, and even gliding through the sky! Let's step into the world of frogs together...

Itzue W. Caviedes Solis

Frogs vs. toads

We share the world with more than 7,000 species of frog. Among them is a family called Bufonidae—these are the "true toads." That means that all toads are frogs, but not all frogs are toads! Frogs and toads share a lot of the same characteristics, so if you come across one of these creatures, you might mistake one for the other. Let's take a look at what makes them different.

Glands

All frogs have glands throughout their skin. Some glands produce mucus to keep the skin moist. Others produce secretions to protect the frogs from microorganisms (tiny living things) and predators.

Frog

Eggs

Most frogs lay their eggs in big clumps. While many frogs lay their eggs in the water, some lay their eggs on leaves, in foam nests, or even carry them on their backs.

Smooth skin

Frogs can breathe through their skin! Their skin also helps them absorb water in order to stay hydrated.

Poisonous glands

Unlike frogs, toads have two parotoid glands, one on each side of the head. When threatened, toads show off their glands and can release toxins from them.

An unusual toad

Just to confuse matters, the purple fluorescent frog belongs to the true toads family, but it looks like a frog! It has smooth skin and no parotoid glands. It is also known as the harlequin toad.

Toad

Bumpy skin

The bumps on a toad's skin are glands (not warts!), which help to reduce water loss. This allows toads to explore dry environments without getting dehydrated.

Toad eggs

Most toads lay their eggs in long jellylike chains, but there are toads that don't lay eggs at all. These toads give birth to tiny toadlets instead!

Sign language

It is noon on the island of Borneo in Southeast Asia. The sun is in the sky, but tall trees are keeping the forest floor cool and shaded. A black-spotted rock frog is relaxing next to a fast-flowing waterfall that splashes all around him.

This habitat might be slippery for some, but the rock frog has no fear! He uses his belly and thighs to **attach to the wet rock**. He has special channels in the skin under his toes and fingers that he uses to get rid of excess water. Clever, huh?

The black-spotted rock frog makes a shrill chirping call, but the waterfall is too loud for the other frogs to hear him. So instead he straightens his leg, opens his toes wide, and waves! He uses his **bright white foot** like a flag to try to attract a female. Sure enough, a frog in the distance raises its foot in response.

This is not the only trick this frog has **evolved** for communicating in a noisy environment. Frogs of this species use a sign language that also includes standing upright, opening their mouth, and even drumming their legs.

One-month-old

One-year-old

The black-spotted rock frog has a white web around its toes that gets brighter as it grows older.

Turning blue

While migrating, males change from beige to dark gray and brown. It is only once they enter the pond that they turn bright blue.

After a **long journey**, a moor frog arrives at a pond in the shallow wetlands of Eastern Austria, Europe. The reason this frog has come to the pond? He is on a quest to find love!

But he has competition... Hundreds of male and female frogs have traveled, or migrated, to the pond and are also looking for a partner. To make sure that he stands out, the brown moor frog jumps in the water and turns **bright blue!**

He doesn't do this to impress the females, but to signal to other males to say, "I am a male frog—don't waste your time trying to impress me!" Seeing the moor frog turn blue, all the other males in the crowded pond know not to follow him. This saves them precious time and effort. The race is on to **impress a female**—may the best frog win!

Suddenly the moor frog spots a female frog by herself on the other side of the pond. Like all females, she is brown. Our frog does not want to miss his chance. He quickly swims toward the female before the other blue males notice. He gets to her first—success! The other male frogs will have to keep looking for a partner.

Super senses

It is a warm, humid afternoon in Suriname, South America. Sunlight barely reaches the bottom of a muddy stream where a Suriname toad is waiting patiently for lunch to swim by. Her flat brown body blends in perfectly with her surroundings, making her almost invisible. The Suriname toad has small eyes and the water is too murky for her to see clearly, but that's not a problem. She has thousands of **sensory receptors** in her body, called neuromasts, that help her feel when prey is close by, even though she can't see anything.

She has no tongue or teeth to catch prey, but that is not a problem either! The Suriname toad senses a fish approaching, opens her mouth wide, and—**SWOOSH!**—she quickly drags in water. The dazzled fish is sucked into her mouth and can't escape, trapped by the toad's long fingers that close the exit like a net. Lunch is served!

Meanwhile... In the hot Australian desert, a turtle frog is burrowed underground, waiting for a thunderstorm to begin...

The toad uses
muscles connected to
her thighs to suck in
and swallow the fish.

You are what you eat

A painted mantella frog is busy having her lunch in a sunny rainforest in Madagascar, an island off the coast of mainland Africa. She crunches across the forest floor looking for arthropods—small invertebrates that have an outer skeleton and a segmented body. Her diet mostly consists of ants, but she won't refuse the occasional mite or millipede. Yummy!

The painted mantella frog doesn't have any teeth, so to catch her food she springs out her tongue and **swallows her prey alive**. Although it's the middle of the day, she roams around without a care in the world because her bright colors warn predators that she is toxic.

The painted mantella frog doesn't produce these toxins herself. Instead, she gets them from the arthropods she eats, especially the mites. This means that after every meal she becomes **more toxic**. But (plot twist!) most of the arthropods don't produce their own toxins either—they get them from the plants they eat. So the toxins pass from a plant, to an arthropod, and finally to the frog. This means that no two painted mantella frogs have the same mixture of toxins. It all depends on what is on the menu where they live!

Scientists still don't know how the toxins are transferred from the painted mantella frog's stomach to her poison glands. Who knows, maybe you will be the one to solve this mystery in the future...

Gliding

Some frogs, such as Wallace's flying frog, can glide through the air between trees! Gliding frogs use the large membranes between their fingers and toes—and skin flaps on their elbows and ankles—to soar with control and direction.

Super swimmers

Aquatic frogs, like the Titicaca water frog, push through water with their large webbed feet. Some species use a breaststroke kick while others alternate their legs.

One foot in front of the other

Frogs that get around by walking, like the bumblebee toad, have slender legs. For each step, they lift their body and alternate opposite arms and legs.

Getting around

Frogs live in many habitats, from hot deserts to tropical rainforests, and from underground all the way up to the tops of the tallest trees. Frogs have different body shapes and ways of moving to escape predators and to find food, shelter, and other frogs.

Going underground

Frogs that burrow, such as the Mexican burrowing toad, have sturdy limbs, small heads, and tiny eyes. Some frogs burrow forward using their hands, while other frogs burrow backward using their feet.

Climbing

Some frogs are excellent climbers. The fringed leaf frog can pull itself up trees and vertical surfaces using its strong grip, combined with large, sticky toe pads.

Leapfrog

Frogs, such as Dumeril's striped frog, jump using their strong hips and legs, then land using their hands. There are other frog species that crash on their face. Ouch!

Some frogs prefer one type of movement, while others use several.

Sunbathing frogs

Up in the canopy of a rainforest in Paraguay, South America, a waxy monkey tree frog is sunbathing! Frogs are **ectotherms**, which means they need external heat to warm up and move. One of the best heat sources is the sun, but most frogs can't sit and relax directly in sunlight because they run the risk of drying out. This is one of the reasons many frogs are nocturnal (active at night).

Frogs have a permeable skin, which allows water to move in and out of their bodies easily. This is useful for staying hydrated, but bad news when the weather becomes too warm.

However, the waxy monkey leaf frog is not like other frogs... The glands behind her eyes produce a **waxy protective substance** that she spreads all over her body using her hands and feet. Her flexible limbs reach every corner of her body—head, arms, legs, belly, and back. After applying this sunscreen, she sits calmly on her favorite vine to soak up the rays!

Besides giving frogs
energy, sunbathing
also helps prevent
fungal infections.

The march of the toads

It is late afternoon and a group of cane toads are resting during their journey across Australia. In 1935, their ancestors were shipped from the Americas to Australia to help farmers, who hoped they would eat beetles that damaged sugar cane crops. But the toads found other animals that were easier to catch.

Now, like previous generations, these cane toads are **migrating** west through hot deserts and cool mountains. Today alone they have traveled the equivalent of two football fields.

Since being in Australia these toads have evolved **larger bodies** and longer back legs. They now also move faster and farther. Today, because they threaten local species, cane toads are seen as a pest and hunted. But the species is still thriving. One of these cane toads alone will soon lay **more than 30,000 eggs!** Her descendants will grow up in around two weeks and keep migrating, each generation stronger than the one before.

Meanwhile... In Borneo, the black-spotted rock frog is waving his leg and inflating his bright white vocal sac to scare away an intruder.

6PM Beware the wolverine

The sun is setting in southern Cameroon, Central Africa, and a couple of hairy frogs, also known as wolverine frogs, are resting among some tree roots. But they're in grave danger. An **unexpected visitor** is approaching...

A human is trying to hunt the wolverine frogs so they can be eaten or sold for money. Many humans think that they can easily hunt frogs because of their small size, but they should think again when it comes to the wolverine frog!

These little guys may seem harmless at first, but they aren't nicknamed wolverines for nothing. All frogs have four fingers and five toes, which are composed of small bones called **phalanges**. The wolverine frogs' secret weapons? They have clawlike phalanges at the tip of their toes.

Sensing the danger, the wolverine frogs make the sharp bones pierce through their skin! The frogs now have **sharp claws**. The wolverine frogs can't feel anything, but these claws can really hurt whoever is attacking them. Eventually, their claws retreat and their skin will heal. These frogs will live to see another day!

The claws are like sharp knives.

Playing dead

A choir of frogs is calling loudly from a swamp in the Atewa Range, East Ghana. Two Ivory Coast running frogs are nearby, walking around the rocky swamp and trying to focus on their own species' calls. This frog has an **ironic name**. You would expect a running frog to mostly *run*, right? Think again! The Ivory Coast running frog prefers to walk. When it needs to run, its steps are uneven—it gallops a little like a horse.

From afar, a curious bird spots one of the frogs. The frogs know they can't outrun the predator, but one of them has a trick up her sleeve to stay safe. When the bird swooshes down, the frog **flips on her back**. She curls her slender arms and legs toward her body to make a ball and remains completely still, her eyes half-closed. She's pretending she's dead! The bird takes a closer look, but because nothing is moving, it flies away uninterested. The frog's strategy of faking death has worked!

Metamorphosis

Frogs are amphibians. Their bodies change dramatically over their lifetimes—from tadpoles that live in water or inside eggs to adult frogs that live on land and breathe air. This process is called metamorphosis. Let's follow a coronated tree frog in the Mexican forest to see what her life cycle looks like!

1. Egg

An unborn frog becomes a tadpole inside a jellylike cover that has no shell. It feeds on the egg's yolk and breathes oxygen through the egg.

2. Tadpole

The tadpole that emerges from the egg can breathe underwater. It swims using its tail.

3. Growing legs

Next, the tadpole starts to grow legs under its tail. They start as small nubs, before developing toes.

4. Growing arms

The tadpole's arms develop inside its body. When fully formed they erupt through the thin skin, one at a time or both at once!

6. Juvenile

The juvenile frog has developed a new mouth and gut. It can stay out of the water, breathing through its skin and newly formed lungs. Its eyes have adjusted to see out of water.

5. Reabsorption

The tadpole reabsorbs its mouth back into its body and won't be able to eat until its mouth and gut change into their adult form. It also reabsorbs its tail to gain valuable nutrients.

In some frog species tadpoles can undergo metamorphosis faster if their pond is drying out.

7. Adult

The frog is now a fully developed adult! Coronated tree frogs undergo metamorphosis in a hole in a tree. Male adults will then find a new hole and call "boop boop boop" to find a female to mate with. Then the cycle starts again!

Underwater dancing

Large webbed feet
help the toads
rotate upside down
and stay balanced.

The male uses his
webbed feet as nets
to gather the eggs.

After a successful afternoon fishing, the Suriname toad has found a dancing partner for the night. Her back skin has been growing thicker, which means she is ready to be a mom. So when a male called her with **clicking sounds** asking her to dance, she agreed.

The male holds the female's waist tightly and they swim toward the surface where they turn over. Floating on their backs, she **lays eggs** that he catches with his belly. Then they dive down, pressing the eggs between them, and turn over again. He gathers the eggs with his legs and rubs them on her back to secure them. After dancing, the female's skin swallows the eggs completely. The frogs will go through metamorphosis inside her, eating egg yolk and breathing oxygen from her blood. When their eyes develop, they will turn toward the light, looking up while finishing the development process.

Not far from the dancing couple is another mom who went though the exact same dance a few months ago and has been carrying tadpoles inside her back ever since. Now, small frogs are **breaking through her skin**, ready to face the world!

The males of this species have a tail.

Tadpoles need to position their heads toward the strong current so they aren't carried away!

Hold on tight!

It is a cold night on Canada's west coast, and a couple of Pacific tailed frogs are leaving the stream where they have been hiding from predators all day. They're hoping to find some tasty insects for dinner.

Pacific tailed frogs have been around for a long time. They belong to one of the **oldest families** in the frog family tree. They don't have tongues or vocal sacs so they don't communicate like other frogs. Instead, they look at each other when sitting on mossy rocks or feel for each other underwater.

While the adults can leave the water to search for food, the tadpoles stay in the **fast-flowing stream**. Aren't they scared of drifting away in the strong current? Not at all! When it comes to navigating these waters, the Pacific tailed frog tadpoles have a superpower.

The tadpoles' teeth are curved, which helps them to grip to rocks.

Their bodies are really flexible so they can withstand even the strongest of currents. To stay in place they flatten their body and attach their mouths to underwater rocks, creating **suction**—as if they were a toilet plunger. To move around, their upper lip moves forward and, once it is fixed, their lower lip follows, just like a caterpillar!

Home sweet leaf

In the rainforests of Colombia, a sun glass frog is hanging upside down under a big heliconia leaf. Can you imagine constantly looking at the world upside down? This frog is used to it! His **adhesive toes** are super sticky, so he is not worried about falling. Over the years he has made this leaf his home, returning to it to call, mate, and care for his eggs.

After the mother laid the eggs, this male was all on his own. He has been keeping a beady eye on his eggs for 24 hours, only taking short breaks to eat. He makes sure to rotate his eggs so that they all grow equally, and he's constantly on the watch for predators. When the eggs hatch as tadpoles, they will **fall into the river below** and dad's job is done!

Even though it's a quiet night, the sun glass frog is not alone. This is a popular neighborhood! Several other males are living under leaves right next to him taking care of their own eggs. Some of the dads have their own leaves, while others share. There's something else cool about these frogs: They have **see-through skin**. This means all of their internal organs are visible to the naked eye—even their beating hearts!

Meanwhile... In the Australian desert, the cane toad is absorbing moisture from the sand through her abdomen. What a smart way to stay hydrated!

Each sun glass frog has a unique combination of yellow spots.

If you look closely, you can see the blood being pumped through a sun glass frog's body!

The pet shop

It's after hours in a pet shop and a small-webbed bell toad is sitting in a glass tank, far away from her home. She used to live in the muddy forests of Vietnam, but last week she was **captured by hunters** and shipped overseas to be sold as a pet. All over the world millions of bell toads are in the same position as this female. The pet shops don't always know where the animals have come from. People like buying these toads for their "fire bellies," but the toads don't have this feature to entertain humans. They have it to ward off predators!

Sometimes, while living in small spaces, frogs can pass one another diseases such as fungal infections. These diseases can be deadly. Amazingly, the small-webbed bell toad can **create her own medicine** using her glands! She uses this medicine to protect herself from infections.

The pet shop opener opens her tank holding a net. The toad puts up a good fight, but with a swift scoop the staff member picks her up—ready to be sent to a new home...

Meanwhile... After his scare earlier, the wolverine frog is having a relaxing night. Floating in a stream, he breathes through the hairlike skin on his body.

Parents

The world can be a tough place, especially for eggs and tadpoles. Some frogs lay hundreds of eggs and never see them again. Others lay fewer eggs, which one or both parents look after to increase their chances of survival. Check out some of these single dads!

Hitching a ride

The dyeing poison frog moistens eggs laid by the female on the forest floor. After hatching, the tadpoles ride on his back! He carries them up to holes in trees high above the ground.

Tadpoles during metamorphosis

A mouthful of frogs

Incredibly, the Darwin's frog carries his tadpoles in his large vocal sac. The tadpoles grow inside, fed by the dad's nutritious secretions through their mouth and skin. Once they have developed into small frogs, they hop out!

Small frogs ready to leave!

Hold on tight!

The common midwife toad wraps his eggs around his legs. Carrying them around means he needs to take shorter jumps. He keeps them wet by swimming and brings them to water when they are ready to hatch.

Mud bath

After the Kumbara night frog mother has laid her eggs on a twig above water, it's time for the dad to enter the scene. He stands on his legs and covers the eggs with mud using his hands. The mud is very good for the eggs—it protects them from predators and keeps them hydrated.

Midnight snack

Under the dark night sky in Uruguay in South America, a Bell's horned frog is on the lookout for something to eat. She mostly eats **vertebrates**—animals that have a backbone. She will happily feed on a frog, a bird, a mouse, or even a snake!

To hunt, she sits quietly and waits for her next victim to pass by. Suddenly she spots a snake sliding down a branch, completely unaware of her. When the snake is close enough, the Bell's horned frog leaps toward it! The frog's mouth is wide open with her **sticky tongue** extended. Will she be able to win this battle?

The snake tries to fight back, but the Bell's horned frog's skull is made of thick bone, which acts as armor to protect her. She also has a **very strong jaw** with curved teeth and some that look like fangs! The snake is unable to escape the Bell's horned frog's bite, who keeps swallowing until the whole snake is in her stomach. Yum!

1AM

Sounds from the underground

It has been raining in Hong Kong, China, for a whole week. The air is hot and moist and filled with the sounds of the big city. An Asian painted frog is walking along the busy streets of this metropolis when she hears a loud **"mooooo"** noise... What could it be?

Don't be fooled—this isn't a herd of cows! It is the call of two male frogs coming from **inside a drain**. The female can also hear a train sliding on its tracks and a bus honking at pedestrians, but she's used to these distractions.

In a big city like Hong Kong, with buildings all around, frogs struggle to find natural bodies of water where they can breed and lay their eggs. These male Asian painted frogs are calling to say they've **found water**. The female is good at navigating the city—she can walk, jump, swim, and climb—and she swiftly finds the males!

Meanwhile... The sun glass frog is back from a stream, where he absorbed water through his abdomen. Now upside down on his leaf again, he is watering his eggs so they don't dry out in the hot weather.

A cozy burrow

It's late in the night and a big thunderstorm that was passing over southwest Australia has finally cleared. The heavy rain has prompted a turtle frog to come out of his burrow. This pink guy has spent most of the year **burrowed underground**. His limbs are short but muscular, especially his arms, which he uses to dig. His underground home is right next to a termite nest, so he always has a quick meal handy!

But now the turtle frog is on a mission—he doesn't want to spend a lot of time above the ground because he likes the comfort of his cozy burrow. He has one thing on his to-do list: **find a partner**. Hoping to attract a female, he inflates his vocal sac and calls loudly: "Croak croak! Croak croak!"

It doesn't take long before the turtle frog finds a female partner. He takes his new companion to his burrow, located 3 ft (1 m) underground. His home is big enough for both of them, and the **moist sand** will keep them cool when the temperature outside gets too hot. Soon they will mate and the female will lay eggs, starting a new family!

In a couple of months, tadpoles will have gone through the entire process of metamorphosis inside their eggs and will be ready to hatch. They will emerge as mini versions of their parents.

The túngara frog's call is a high-pitched "whine, chuck, chuck, chuck."

Midges are also listening to the frog's call. They want to feed on his blood!

Dangers in the night

It's a quiet and peaceful night in the forests of Panama, Central America, and the túngara frog is floating in a shallow pond. He is calling to attract a female's attention. When calling, his vocal sac inflates and creates **ripples in the water** around him. Other male frogs can hear him and feel the ripples in the water, so they call even louder to compete! But there is another listener too...

A fringe-lipped bat heard the loud chorus and senses a possible meal. She is able to find the frog because she uses **echolocation**, sending out sound waves from her nose that bounce back to her when they hit something. So even though it's pitch black, she knows the exact location of the frog and swooshes down. When he notices the bat approaching at full speed, the túngara frog quickly slips behind a clump of grass. That was a narrow escape! The túngara frog waits for a few minutes before making his way back to the pond, wondering what else the night will bring.

Meanwhile... The snake wasn't enough, so the hungry Bell's horned frog is now devouring a mouse!

Glossary

Amphibian
An animal that has cold blood, bones, and spends part of its life in water (inside an egg or outside in a pond or stream) and part on land. Amphibians include frogs, salamanders, and caecilians.

Aquatic
Used to describe organisms (including animals and plants) that live in water.

Arthropod
An animal with no bones and an external skeleton made of keratin (the same material as your hair and nails). Insects and spiders are arthropods.

Breeding
The act of reproducing to make babies.

Burrow
A hole or tunnel that has been dug underground.

Ectotherm
An animal that does not produce its own heat.

Gland
A part of a body that produces chemical substances.

Metamorphosis
The process of transformation between different life stages, for example a tadpole turning into a frog.

Migration
The movement of animals from one place to another.

Phalanges
Small bones that make up the individual sections of fingers and toes.

Predator
An animal that hunts and eats other animals.

Prey
An animal that is hunted and eaten by other animals.

Tadpole
The aquatic form young frogs and toads take before they turn into adults.

True toad
Frogs that belong to the family Bufonidae.

Vocal sac
Skin under a frog's chin that can be inflated. Frogs can use their vocal sacs to call or to perform visual signals.

Index

Species list

Frogs vs. toads:
Frog: *Heterixalus rutenbergi*
Toad: *Telmatobufo bullocki*
Upper right: *Atelopus hoogmoedi*

12PM: *Staurois parvus*
1PM: *Rana arvalis*
2PM: *Pipa pipa*
3PM: *Mantella baroni*

Getting around:
Burrower: *Rhinophrynus dorsalis*
Glider: *Rhacophorus nigropalmatus*
Walker: *Melanophryniscus stelzneri*
Swimmer: *Telmatobius culeus*
Climber: *Cruziohyla craspedopus*
Jumper: *Leptodactylus gracilis*

4PM: *Phyllomedusa sauvagii*
5PM: *Rhinella marina*
6PM: *Trichobatrachus robustus*
7PM: *Kassina arboricola*

Metamorphosis: *Anotheca spinosa*

8PM: *Pipa pipa*
9PM: *Ascaphus truei*
10PM: *Hyalinobatrachium aureoguttatum*
11PM: *Bombina microdeladigitora*

Parents:
A mouthful of frogs: *Rhinoderma darwinii*
Mud bath: *Nyctibatrachus kumbara*
Hold on tight: *Alytes obstetricans*
Hitching a ride: *Dendrobates tinctorius*

12AM: *Ceratophrys ornata*
1AM: *Kaloula pulchra*
2AM: *Myobatrachus gouldii*
3AM: *Engystomops pustulosus*

This has been a

NEON  SQUID

production

To the frogs, thank you for existing, for filling my life with much joy, and for introducing me to amazing places and people.

To my family, who encouraged me to read since I was little and unconditionally supported my love for frogs.

To my husband, my favorite science communicator.

Author: Itzue W. Caviedes Solis
Illustrator: Henry Rancourt

Editorial Assistant: Malu Rocha
US Editor: Allison Singer Kushnir
Proofreader: Laura Gilbert